THE CONFIDENT CATECHIST

Dedication

To my husband, Michael

Author Acknowledgments

I would like to acknowledge the support of my family, Becca, Beth, Alex, Dereck, Sarah, Ben, and Lexi; the Clusterettes of the Archdiocese of Boston; and my editor, Laurie Delgatto.

THE CONFIDENT CATECHIST

STRATEGIES FOR THE NEW AND NOT-SO-NEW VOLUNTEER

Lee Danesco

saint mary's press

The publishing team included Laurie Delgatto, development editor; Lorraine Kilmartin, reviewer; prepress and manufacturing coordinated by the prepublication and production services departments of Saint Mary's Press.

Printed in the United States of America

3830

ISBN 978-0-88489-961-7

Library of Congress Cataloging-in-Publication Data

Danesco, Lee.
The confident catechist : strategies for the new and not-so-new volunteer / Lee Danesco.
p. cm.
ISBN 978-0-88489-961-7 (pbk.)
1. Catechists. 2. Christian education—Teacher training. 3. Christian educators. I. Title.
BX1918.D36 2007
268'.3—dc22

2006012736

Contents

Introduction

Faith teaching and sharing is more than simply transmitting information from one person to another. It requires more than directing young people to read pages and answer questions. As catechist and ministry volunteers, we need to know how to approach young people, how to involve them, and how to organize them in ways that enhance their comprehension, encourage their participation, and enrich their spirituality. *The Confident Catechist: Strategies for the New and Not-So-New Volunteer* is a practical response to these very real needs. It helps volunteers bridge the gap between knowing what to teach and knowing how to teach it.

The Confident Catechist includes ten independently written articles geared toward improving the faith-sharing skills of religious education and youth ministry volunteers. Each article explores a specific teaching tool, technique, or outlook. The techniques are not revolutionary or trendy; they are classic and have withstood the test of time in faith-sharing settings.

Reflective questions following each offering help the volunteers apply the message to their own ministry and teaching experience. Designed for time-conscious, results-oriented volunteers (like you!), the articles are compact, direct, and easily read in a single sitting. Because each article can stand alone, no background or preliminary reading is required. Simply select a topic and begin to help yourself to more productive faith-sharing sessions.

A Winning Beginning

This is your first day teaching a religious education class. Not only have you never taught a religion class, but you've never taught *anything* to a group of young people. How will you begin?

Or maybe it's your first day teaching this year. You may have led faith-sharing groups for several years now, but each year it seems a little more difficult to start off on the right foot. Maybe this year will be different. How will you begin?

Could it really be your twelfth or thirteenth first-day experience? Sometimes you feel like you have been sharing faith with young people forever. What will you do this year to keep from boring them and yourself? How will you begin?

Because each religious education situation is unique, there are as many good ways to begin a faith-sharing year as there are adult ministry leaders. But all catechist and ministry volunteers facing a new beginning can better direct their energy and improve the likelihood of a successful start with the help of the following basic do's and don'ts.

Do Plan to Make a Good First Impression

The first gathering you have with a new group of young people can be filled with unknowns. You don't know them. They don't know you. They may not even know one another very well. And no one knows what lies ahead. By making a good first impression, you can relieve the tension of the moment and lay a solid foundation for the remainder of the year. But how do you step into a scenario of such uncertainty and project the image of a calm and competent leader? Plan!

Of course, you will want to familiarize yourself with the objectives of the lesson and review the steps and materials you will use to achieve those objectives in advance. But planning can also mean getting to know about the young people in the group before you ever meet them. An advanced look at a class list can tell you if the group is gender balanced, neighborhood concentrated, or ethnically diverse. Your director of religious education (DRE) or coordinator of youth ministry (CYM) can provide you with helpful information about the young people in the group who may have learning issues or special physical or emotional needs. Being aware of these factors from the beginning can help you relate quickly and sensitively to the faith-sharing potential of the young people in your group.

Finally, the more you know about the teaching environment, the more comfortable you can be. This makes it essential to check out, in advance, the contours and seating arrangement of the meeting space; the location of supply closets, restrooms, and fire exits; and how you can reach the DRE or CYM. By investing just a little time in this kind of advanced planning, you can make a first impression that will help ease the first-day jitters and help you establish a good rapport with your group.

Don't Think a Bad First Impression Can Never Be Reversed

What if the first gathering isn't all you had hoped for? Be ready to put it in proper perspective. Look at the calendar. See how many more opportunities there will be for you to improve on whatever your first impression might have lacked. One meeting is just that—a single opportunity to share faith. There will be more.

When the first gathering is over, make it a learning tool you can use to improve your efforts. Replay your time with the young people slowly in your mind, pausing and focusing on the good things that happened and making note of successful techniques or approaches you might repeat. You can also reflect on the need for changes by considering what didn't work at all and what might work better if you make some adjustments. Then do what most of the young people did ten minutes after the meeting ended—move on.

Do Announce the Basic Code of Conduct

Are you a tough disciplinarian, a laid-back freewheeler, or someone happily in between? Surprisingly, more important than your management style is your ability to explain clearly what you expect of the group. The first meeting presents the perfect opportunity for you to set out for the young people, in kind but firm language, the basic code of conduct that will help everyone experience a pleasant, productive climate for faith sharing. You might even consider involving the young people in developing a code of conduct. The rules should reflect the general rules of the parish and align with diocesan policies. Of course, the common theme that underlies appropriate behavior at any religious education or youth ministry gathering or event is always Christian respect.

To provide the kind of atmosphere in which spiritual development can happen, the code of conduct should ensure that everyone will be respectful by paying attention, following directions, and maintaining quiet when asked to do so. Perhaps more difficult, the rules should lead the young people to respect themselves by acting in ways that show they value who they are and what they are doing. You can complete the circle of respect by modeling actions and reactions that acknowledge the dignity and importance you assign to each member of the group.

Young people can relax and work to their potential when they feel comfortable about who is in charge and know what is expected of them. You can relax and work to your potential when you know you have set ground rules that maximize everyone's opportunity to grow in the faith.

Don't Be Afraid to Discipline

When you meet your group of young people for the first time, you will instinctively want to like them, and it is likely that they will feel the same way toward you. But it may not be long before that mutual good feeling is interrupted by someone's forgetfulness, willfulness, unruliness, or just plain silliness. Your reaction to those early challenges to the established rules should reflect your recognition that the young people are coming to you from many different backgrounds and experiences. Some will already have built-in behavior codes; others will not. Some will make mistakes, speak out of turn, and not be predisposed to cooperate or share. And everyone will be experiencing the inherent awkwardness that comes with being part of a new group.

It is appropriate to temper your discipline with good humor, patience, and common sense, but it is essential to be ready and willing to curb and correct inappropriate behavior. This may mean taking a firm stand with a firm voice, restricting activities, rearranging seats, or denying privileges. It may even mean speaking individually with certain young people about their behavior or working with the DRE or CYM for further disciplinary actions.

We all hope our gatherings will run smoothly with no disciplinary issues, but we all know this will rarely be the case. When difficulties do arise, you may feel reluctant to discipline for fear of alienating a young person. This is a normal reaction, but as the group leader, your primary responsibility is to maintain a safe and enjoyable learning environment for all the young people in the group. Knowing your disciplinary options and applying them calmly, consistently, and fairly will enable you to provide the kind of environment where everyone can enjoy faith-sharing experiences.

Do Make That First Lesson Enjoyable

There is no rule that says learning activities have to be boring. Our faith tells us that we are sharing the most joyful news imaginable. Our lessons, and the manner in which we share them, should reflect that truth.

As a catechist or ministry volunteer, you will likely be expected to follow the direction of your DRE or CYM and share an assigned lesson each time you gather with your group of young people. But lessons and sessions are often simply words on a page. You are the one who can bring that lesson to life and make it seem important to the group, so you must consider in advance how you can enliven and personalize the first session and all the sessions that follow.

What can you say or do to help illuminate the lesson's central truth? What can you add to the lesson to make it real? What part of you can you contribute to this session—a personal story, a photo, a relevant prayer? How can you lead the young people to connect this lesson to their own lives? Squarely confronting questions like these in advance can help you see the lesson from the group's perspective and make it more user friendly.

Don't Make the First Lesson a Three-Ring Circus

It is natural for you to want to stir up interest and excitement, especially at your first gathering. By looking in resource books or going online, you can find hundreds of fun-filled activity ideas that can add creative dimensions to any meeting. Used properly and sparingly, these teaching tools can help you actively engage the young people. But don't get caught up in your own first-session enthusiasm. If given the option to add such activities to an assigned session, select something simple, time-efficient, and relevant to the lesson. An over-the-top beginning can put you in the unenviable position of needing to produce something spectacular each week, an added pressure that no catechist or ministry volunteer needs to take on. Don't actively seek complications.

Some Closing Thoughts

Whether you are a rookie or a veteran, lots of advice will come your way. Everyone will have a suggestion for you about how to begin. Listen to it all, consider it all, but don't get caught up in it all. Don't worry that you don't know everything there is to know about working with young people. No one does. If you center on these few simple do's and don'ts and rely on your faith and God's love, you and the young people will have the winning beginning you deserve.

Think About . . .

1. Try to recall the emotions you experienced as a young person when you were meeting a group of strangers or beginning a new activity. How did you hope the group leader would treat you? Given the ages of the young people you are working with, what unique kinds of fears are they likely to feel? What can you do to minimize their apprehensions?
2. As a catechist or ministry volunteer, what are you most confident about? most concerned about?
3. What three rules will be the most important for you to share with the young people? Think about how you will explain those rules in age-appropriate language and with relevant examples.

Finding Your Focus

You are only a few minutes into a session, and already you are struggling to maintain eye contact with the group. Some of the young people are still listening, but many are visually surveying the room for diversions, and one seems about ready to nod off. What can you do to get the young people back on track, connect them to the lesson, and improve their understanding of its contents? You are ready to try almost anything. How about a focus? A focus can be any word or object that, when centrally placed, draws and holds the attention of the group while clarifying and enriching the meaning of the lesson.

Focus Approaches

Group focus approaches are limited in scope and number only by your imagination, sense of humor, patience, and, of course, the developmental level and understanding of the young people in the group. Following are some of the more conventional focus types.

Simple-Word Focus

The most common focus technique is one you may already be using. You may use the simple-word approach by writing a word or phrase on a chalkboard, a whiteboard, or a sheet of newsprint at the beginning of the session.

The word or phrase should announce the main topic or theme of the session. For example, if the day's lesson centers on the Lord's Prayer, write "Lord's Prayer" on the board or newsprint. During the session, occasionally return to those words, underlining them, starring them, circling them, and even drawing arrows toward them for repeated emphasis. The words provide an anchor for the young people, keeping their attention on the lesson securely in place. Looking at the board anytime throughout the session will bring the young people back to the main idea of the day's lesson. This simple-word focus can help ensure that every young person will leave the session firmly attached to the central message for the day.

Consider varying the way you present the focus words—in bold print, in small italicized print, on colored sheets of paper, on a banner, on a T-shirt, on a balloon, or even on a large sheet cake. You might even give each young person an index card or a small slip of paper with the focus word written on it. The possibilities are as exciting as you wish to make them.

Visuals

Putting words on the board works, but this method works better if it is used in rotation with other focus tools. Fortunately, there are many. Maps, charts, graphs, and photographs can be wonderful focal points when you connect them to a lesson and refer to them throughout the session to further develop or enrich a point.

A map of the ancient Middle East can help the young people more clearly visualize and locate the scene of any Gospel story. Colorful charts or graphs can attract attention to, and provide clear explanation of, a simple analysis of the growth of the

Catholic Church over time. And, of course, photos of a recent parish Baptism, Confirmation, or First Communion provide a personal way to connect the young people with the sacramental life discussed in a text.

Whatever visual you select, be sure to maximize the results it can produce by placing it where the young people can easily see it—on a board, on a shared table, duplicated in various locations, or occasionally even passed around the room. Then remember to reference the focus repeatedly throughout the session. Simply displaying a visual device and making only a passing reference to it is ineffective and may actually distract the group.

The Unexpected

Perhaps the focus tools you will enjoy most are those you gather from your own surroundings. You can use everyday items like a rock, a can of soda, or a sack of potatoes to make connections to lesson topics and themes. Rocks of different sizes, placed in appropriate locations, can provide compelling images for lessons that discuss the martyrdom of Stephen or the woman caught in adultery. With just a little direction and imagination, the young people can picture the rock that is sitting on their table as one of those raised against Stephen or the adulterous woman. Being able to pick up the rock, touch it, imagine the pain of being struck by it, brings the young people more clearly into the Scripture event.

A can of soda might provide a link to topics like the gifts of the Holy Spirit that are waiting within us to bubble forth. It might also become a tool for talking about stewardship of the land through recycling. A shaken can of soda provides a focus for talking about our bottled-up human emotions and how explosive they could become.

The obvious use of the potato sack is as a focus for discussion on world hunger. By removing the potatoes and distributing them around the room, you provide tangible proof of how the world's goods are unevenly distributed, some people randomly receiving large potatoes, others small potatoes, some none at all. But the individual potatoes in the sack can also demonstrate how unique we are as human beings, no two potatoes (or humans) being the same.

Potluck

When the young people are comfortable with the use of a focus, you might want to recruit them to provide some of their own focus materials. When you announce the topic for an upcoming lesson, ask for volunteers to bring objects from their own homes or yards that they think will help focus everyone on the lesson for the week. The benefit here, of course, is threefold: you get help with providing a focus, the volunteers have to do some real thinking about the topic and may begin to look at everyday items as possible spiritual tools, and you coincidentally stimulate the young people's curiosity and interest in an upcoming theme or topic.

Some Closing Thoughts

Not all young people come to faith-sharing sessions with well-developed verbal skills. Some may show a positive attitude toward the faith but can be turned off, or away, by traditional textbook approaches to learning. If your approach includes simple-word, visual, unexpected, or potluck focus items that help make learning clear, concrete, or tactile, you can draw everyone in and provide a lesson that the young people can take home.

Think About . . .

1. Look around the room you are in right now. What is the focus point of each side or corner of the room? Where do your eyes go and linger or return? What is the focus point of each of your rooms at home?
2. Have you already used a focus as a teaching tool with your group of young people? If so, what was the focus and how did it assist your teaching efforts? What worked well? not so well?
3. Suppose the main topic for an upcoming session is one of those listed here. What focus ideas would you use for each?
   - prayer
   - the Eucharist
   - the story of the good Samaritan
4. Consider possible uses for the focus items listed here. What faith-related topics might connect well with these objects?
   - a plate of cookies
   - a flower
   - a throw pillow
   - a book

Making the Most of Motion

Are you one of the many catechist and ministry volunteers who share the recurring nightmare of young people constantly moving around, helter-skelter, out of control at every gathering? Are you anxious in the presence of too many moving parts and not enough order? Do you find yourself compelled to intervene and put a halt to motion of almost any kind?

A more realistic approach might be for you to see motion not as a hazard but as a potential tool, one you already use in your own daily life. You certainly understand the value of taking a walk, alternating tasks, or relocating to different workspaces to reduce tedium and refocus your thinking. You have learned through experience that this kind of intermittent motion makes you better at, and happier about, whatever it is you are doing.

You can apply this same positive attitude to motion in faith-sharing sessions with equal success. Once you accept the need to stop swimming against the tide of youthful energy, you can learn and apply the teaching techniques that will help you harness that powerful current for productive ends.

The Techniques of Motion

Every faith-sharing setting has three easily distinguishable moveable parts: a leader, equipment, and young people. All motion and motion techniques necessarily stem from one of these sources.

Moving the Leader

The least complicated technique, moving the leader, invites you to introduce motion by assuming a variety of postures throughout a faith-sharing session. For example, you can move from a sitting position to a standing position to indicate that you are about to change topics. The exaggerated steps you suddenly take toward individuals or small groups can reinforce a concept or lend intensity to a question. Even slowly and quietly taking a seat can help you announce a moment of reflection or a time for group prayer.

If you are dramatically inclined, you may feel comfortable introducing more elaborate gestures when sharing a story or reading from the Scriptures. If you have a large meeting space, you may feel totally at ease moving from the front of the space to the back, or in smaller areas equally comfortable moving slowly around a table. But even without such extensive motion, you can energize yourself and the young people by learning to effectively change postures while leading a session.

When you get up out of a chair and become physically involved in the lesson, you truly come alive. Your facial expressions, pattern of speech, and mood all respond to the therapy of movement. Caught up vicariously in your motion, a group will respond to a new, energized you. A lesson instantly becomes animated.

Moving Equipment

To add to the sense of motion you create by your own actions, you can regularly enlist the help of the young people in chores that require them to get up and move. The young people will gladly move chairs to clusters for small-group discussions, to pairs for peer activities, or to the perimeter of the room to create an open area for doing crafts or giving presentations.

Redesigning the learning space will result in a few moments of noise and confusion. But for the young people, both the act of moving the furniture and their own relocation in the room will help defuse their natural restlessness and allow them to settle in for whatever comes next.

Fortunately, young people can derive similar benefits by moving considerably less cumbersome equipment. Anyone who has watched a young person pass a note knows that half the fun is in the actual passing, because action is involved. By liberally requiring the act of "passing" throughout a learning activity, you can encourage the kind of motion that helps keep young people engaged.

One simple activity that creatively uses "passing" is the review of any well-known story, such as that of the good Samaritan. In this activity, you ask the young people to begin to write the story in their own words. For variety they can begin to draw a picture of the story. After a few moments, say "pass" and have all the young people pass their papers in a predetermined direction. Each young person then continues to write or draw the story from the point where the previous writer or artist left off. This sequential writing and passing continues until the stories are completed and then shared.

With each act of passing, the young people are reinvigorated and feel participatory rather than combative. Whether the young people are passing markers, books, or snacks, the positive expenditure of energy ripples around the room. For you, motion can become an enabler of, and not a deterrent to, sharing the faith.

Moving the Young People

The most challenging movement is that done by the young people themselves. Fortunately, there are many resources available to assist catechists in selecting age-appropriate skits, crafts, relays, and other learning activities that get young people moving. But don't be afraid to design your own. Let the young people act out parts of a lesson, move into pairs and interview each other, or sit in small groups and produce a community craft.

If space permits, you might build motion into your session by asking the young people to move from one previously established learning or activity station to another on a rotating schedule. Although creating such a session requires some advanced planning, providing the opportunity to move everyone from one fresh venue to another several times during a session is well worth the effort.

Group discussion provides less structured opportunities for moving the young people. Formatting questions that have no right or wrong answer will help get everyone involved. For example, you might ask an opinion question like "How many of you think . . ." or a question of choice like "How many of you are more like Saint Peter than you are like Saint Paul?" By asking the young people to respond to such non-threatening questions in creative ways such as raising two hands, standing up, or clapping, you can open the door to motion and cooperative learning.

Sometimes, of course, even your best efforts to create motion just aren't enough. In those few instances, you might want to introduce the 60-second break. This technique allows everyone to stand up, talk, and move around the meeting space with the understanding that in exactly sixty seconds, everyone must be ready to physically and mentally regroup and return to task. On days before or after holidays, on rainy days, or on any day when the room seems ready to burst, a 60-second break is a minute very well spent.

Some Closing Thoughts

The success of motion as a teaching technique rests on its implementation. Begin with the understanding that what you try should be governed by the age and make-up of the group. Are the young people in the group chatty or quiet, friendly or shy, responsive or resistant? and what about the meeting space? How much room do you have to work with and what special features must you consider? Forcing even the best method to work in an inappropriate setting is likely to prove frustrating for all.

As willing as you may be to give motion a try, don't try every technique at once. It is good to bring some movement into each gathering, but there is no need to bring all types of motion into every gathering. As you introduce new techniques, vary your approach. Do not overuse particular methods, because any technique that is used too often will lose its appeal and effectiveness. Besides, there are countless ways to create movement and little need to get bogged down with two or three personal favorites.

Motion techniques are most effective when they are an integrated part of the teaching plan. In your search for effective motion techniques, always look for those that advance a teaching goal.

Finally, motion is most definitely not the only tool you need to successfully manage your group. But the next time you are trying to teach a group of young people who want to learn but who don't want to sit still, making the most of their motion may be the best place for you to start.

Think About . . .

1. Think about a previous session. How much time did you spend sitting down? standing? moving around? How might you have better balanced your use of these different postures?
2. At a previous session, did you include the movement of any equipment or of the young people themselves? If so, how? If not, how might you add motion to that lesson?
3. Give some thought to the space where you gather. What constructive changes in seating could you reasonably make? How do you think an occasional change in the seating arrangement might affect the young people? How would it affect your teaching style?

Questions, Questions, Questions

They can be as short as "What's up?" or as annoying as "Are we there yet?" Some, such as "What time is it?" are meant to gather information. Others, like "Don't you know any better?" are delivered rhetorically to make a point. However they are used, questions are a regular part of our everyday conversations. When used creatively by catechist and ministry volunteers, questions can make a real difference in faith sharing because they help young people listen, think, and respond.

Unlike simple declarative sentences, which can quickly blur to a monotonous drone, questions invade young people's consciousness with the compelling tone of an unrelenting wake-up call. The challenge of the question is clearly extended to everyone in a group. No one gets a pass. Everyone's attention is required.

By actively pushing the issue, questions function as more than just attention getters. They also provide a provocative, straight-forward call to real intellectual activity. Questions direct young people to connect what they are being asked to what they already know, to turn the question and their existing knowledge around together in their minds until they get a fit. Questions encourage young people to reflect, evaluate, consider, decide, think. Questions move the mind.

Three Kinds of Questions

As you consider how to incorporate the power of questions into faith-sharing sessions, you will recognize that not all questions are the same.

Fact questions ask for specific, concrete information and allow for a very limited number of possible correct answers. Usually, fact questions begin with words like *who, what, why, when, where* or *how.* Fact questions require the young people to tap into their memories and respond on the basis of what they already know. An example of a fact question is this: Where was Jesus baptized?

Opinion questions seek answers that often rely more upon personal preferences and thinking than upon fact. Because these questions do not require factual responses, the range of possible correct answers is wide. It is important, however, to note that some opinions are the result of a person's analysis of the facts—an opinion about war, for example. Opinion questions usually include words like *you* or *your* and seek a personal, more feeling-based response. An example of an opinion question is this: How would you feel about being baptized in a river?

Hypothetical questions combine elements of fact and opinion questions. They direct the young people to produce a response to a prepared scenario by relying on facts as well as personal experience. Hypothetical questions ask responders to evaluate a situation and make a decision. Often hypothetical questions begin with words like *suppose* or *imagine.* An example of a hypothetical question is this: Suppose you were told that you were going to be baptized in a river. How would you prepare for this event?

As the leader of the group, you can direct each of these types of questions toward the young people in a variety of ways. You can ask the questions verbally or in written form. You can solicit individual responses or a group response. You can distribute prepared questions and let the young people quiz one another. You might even encourage the young people to create their own questions on a given topic for use among themselves or to be directed to you or other ministry leaders.

Using the Questions

As with any teaching tool, questions can be very effective if you learn how to vary them throughout a session and throughout the year. You may want to consider the following suggestions for using questions during each of the four key junctures of any faith-sharing session.

Review

At the start of a religious education or ministry session, it is often helpful to reconnect everyone to information shared at the previous session. Structuring this initial review around a series of questions will not only help the young people remember previous lessons but will also draw them back into the learning process and their own faith-sharing community.

You might start with a very general opinion question like, "So, who remembers what we were talking about the last time we met?" If more specific fact questions seem in order, use a chalkboard, a whiteboard, or a sheet of newsprint to display several key words from the previous lesson. Allow for brief informal sharing among the young people and then ask, "Who can tell us the meaning of any one of these words and how we used it in the previous session?" Complete the review by repeating this question until the group has defined and discussed all the words.

If occasionally the group requires an even more structured approach, distribute three short written questions based on the previous lesson. Ask the young people to work individually or in pairs and then to share their responses with the group.

Lesson Introduction

The beginning of a new lesson is an ideal time to use non-threatening opinion questions that the young people can respond to with a simple show of hands. For example, if a lesson focuses on the sacrament of Penance and Reconciliation, you might ask questions that begin, "How many of you have ever . . ." You might end a question like this with "asked someone to forgive you?", "done something you were sorry for later?", or "wanted a chance to start over?" Used like this, questions can help ease everyone into the lesson by connecting them with the topic in a personal way.

You can also use introductory questions to ask the young people to write down or share a specific number of things they already know or don't know about a new topic. If the day's lesson is about the sacrament of Confirmation, why not begin by asking, "What are three things you already know about Confirmation?" or "What two questions do you have about Confirmation that you hope we will answer today?" The young people can share their questions out loud or submit them in written form. Again, the goal of the questions is not only to introduce the topic but also to invite everyone into the learning process.

Lesson Development

Even if you feel comfortable using questions to review or introduce topics, when it is time to present the core of the lesson, you may experience an urgency to do much more telling and far less asking. Telling the young people the lesson is an attractive option, because it allows you to gallop through pages of material and finish the lesson fairly quickly. The downside is that under a constant barrage of declarative sentences, the young people will begin to zone out and you will soon discover you are galloping alone. Questions can help you avoid that disaster. Consider interrupting your presentation periodically with questions that will lure the young people out of their glazed-over state and back into the lesson. Or try nonthreatening opinion questions like, "So what do you think about what I have said so far?" or "What surprises you most about what I have said?" or even "What do you think we are going to discuss next?" These kinds of questions say to everyone, "I know you're out there, I want your feedback, and I believe you can help me share the faith."

As you develop a lesson, you might decide to vary the tempo or mood of the session by challenging the group to resolve a related hypothetical question. Although developing hypothetical questions may add some time to your preparation, you'll find that the resulting level of involvement and participation is well worth the effort.

Lesson Conclusion

As you draw lessons to a close, don't forget how helpful questions can be in providing a restatement of the main concepts shared. Now is the time to make good use of the traditional, factual review questions found in most religious education books. Discussing such questions allows the young people to demonstrate how well they learned the lesson, and it also allows you to evaluate what points you might need to reinforce or correct. You might also choose to build a summary around a general opinion question such as, "For you, what was the most important thing we talked about today?"

As always, the opinion question has no correct answer, so it opens the door to universal participation. But in this case, it also requires the young people to actively reflect on the time shared and fix their minds on a definite response. Summarizing the lesson through questions and answers allows the young people to participate in naming and securing what they have learned.

Your guidance at this juncture is crucial in helping the young people see the important distinction between the personal opinions they may have shared and Church teaching, which remains unchanged.

Some Closing Thoughts

Do you think questions could help you be a more effective leader? How can questions help you outline content, frame the learning process, and enliven learning sessions? Can questions lead you to connect directly with the young people and share their excitement in discovering the faith? How can the young people learn as much from what you ask them as from what you tell them? Questions, questions, questions.

Think About . . .

1. Think about how you greet the young people who gather with you. What questions are already a regular part of your time together? How can you expand or modify those questions for better results?

2. If you were preparing to share a previous lesson again, how might you use additional questions in the development section of the session?
3. As you look at the lesson topics for the next few weeks, what occasions do you see for the young people to question one another? for written questions? for other creative question activities?

Holding Their Attention

One of the least enjoyable but most necessary elements of faith sharing with young people is managing wandering minds and fidgeting bodies. A natural way to establish your teaching authority is to announce a list of rules and explain the consequences for breaking them. Unfortunately, the problem with relying totally on rules to maintain order is that enforcing them can often mean interrupting the flow of a lesson.

Thankfully, there is another way. What if instead of focusing on rules and consequences, you concentrate your efforts on teaching lessons that are so compelling and so engaging that you seldom need mention the rules? You can find working examples of this approach to group management in the scriptural accounts of the teaching ministry of Jesus.

During his public ministry, Jesus attracted large, diverse crowds of curious onlookers. As with many religious education and youth ministry events, each crowd included its own unique collection of potentially disruptive personalities. Jesus faced everything from political activists to religious fanatics, from the marginalized to the privileged. All gathered with great curiosity around the young rabbi.

How was Jesus able to reach and teach such challenging audiences? What did he say or do to make these mixed multitudes want to listen? Jesus held his would-be disciples in check by successfully applying teaching techniques that, with a little adaptation, you can also use to lead young Christian disciples today.

Have an Important Message That Targets Your Audience

Jesus captured and kept the attention of his listeners because he had something important to say just to them. He preached the good news of salvation and the coming of the Reign of God. His words of hope seemed to be a direct response to the spiritual needs and longings of his Jewish audience, people suffering the misery of Roman occupation. Because his message related to them, when Jesus spoke, his listeners fell still, their petty arguments temporarily forgotten, the daily gossip put on hold. They listened intently as Jesus brought them a powerful message of peace, joy, forgiveness, and love and placed it squarely in the context of their daily lives.

For catechist and ministry volunteers, having an important message means coming to grips with the core ideas of each lesson and committing yourself to sharing those ideas to the best of your ability. Just like the adult crowds who followed Jesus, the young people can and will recognize the difference between a leader who confidently arrives with something to say and one who is there just to pass the time. The first will win their respect and attention; the second will not.

As you share a lesson, focus on connecting the message to the daily lives of the young people gathered. For example, try comparing prayer to an online chat with a good friend, or the Ten Commandments to the school behavior code. The more successful you are at relating the message to the young people—their interests, their problems, their relationships, their future—the more likely they are to listen and get involved, and the less likely you are to have disciplinary issues.

Make Good Use of All Available Teaching Tools

When we read scriptural accounts of Jesus's teaching the crowds, we know that he was sharing his message without the use of a television, a DVD, or even a basic textbook. How did he manage? He fashioned teaching tools out of what was available to him: objects from everyday life, the imagination of his listeners, and the varied environment around him. Jesus helped his audience stay focused by teaching with familiar, concrete examples taken from daily living. For instance, instead of just talking to a group of people about the beauty of childlike faith, Jesus set a young child in their midst and so brought his message to life. When questioned about paying taxes to the emperor, Jesus avoided a long theological discussion, electing instead to use the well-known Roman coin to illustrate his response. Other visual aids Jesus used included common items like wheat, fish, bread, sheep, and wine, but immersed in his message, each item took on new meaning and significance and each caught the attention of the crowds.

Jesus also used the imaginations of his followers to help him teach. As he asked provocative questions and wove colorful stories, he called upon his followers to create their own accompanying mental images, which both enriched and personalized his teachings. Potential malcontents didn't become disruptive; they were too busy picturing a man going down to Jericho who fell in with robbers, or a son taking his inheritance and spending it irresponsibly, or a woman tearing her house apart to find a missing coin.

Finally, Jesus knew how to use and tailor the available teaching environments to keep his message alive. He didn't confine his preaching to one synagogue or one town. He was constantly on the move, speaking in Capernaum, Naim, Bethsaida, wherever a crowd gathered. When a change in venue might improve a lesson, Jesus willingly taught from a boat, in a garden, on a mountainside, in an upper room, along a dusty road, even from the cross. Jesus taught in an age that was technologically deficient, but he never lacked for teaching devices. He simply made good use of whatever he had.

You can do what Jesus did. You can use concrete focus items, draw on the imagination of your group, and vary the faith-sharing environment. But in the twenty-first century, you can also do much more. In today's multimedia world, you can select teaching aids from an endless array of videos, DVDs, music, crafts, skits, and projects.

To maintain optimum effectiveness, vary the tools you use, use only what enhances the message, and let go of strategies that don't work for you. By carefully selecting and implementing the best tools available, you can add new dimensions of interest and excitement to sessions and keep the young people on task and out of trouble.

Teach with Compassion

Jesus's ministry shows that having an important message, appropriately targeting the audience, and creatively employing teaching tools are not always enough to keep people interested. Jesus had days when people just didn't get the message and days when they got the message but didn't like it. There were even days when crowds murmured, protested, or simply walked away. Jesus found their lack of understanding annoying, frustrating, and perhaps even infuriating.

But he didn't give up on people; instead Jesus continued to teach his message through daily acts of caring and compassion. Even reluctant followers watched and marveled as Jesus gently cured the sick, the blind, and the lame. They stood in awe as he lovingly mingled in community with the poor, the outcasts, and the sinners. They were touched by the tears he shed over the loss of a friend. Perhaps as much as his message or his teaching tools, it was Jesus's compassion for the people that drew and held their hearts and minds.

Leading with compassion means having patience, showing kindness, refraining from sarcasm or meanness, and treating each young person as you would want your own children to be treated. It means asking how someone is feeling and really caring about his or her response. It means remembering the special things that are going on in the lives of the young people in your group—rejoicing in the good times and offering support in the bad. It means reaching out in a personal way to each person every time you gather.

Consistently sharing your compassion in these simple ways can lay the foundation for respect and trust among those you teach.

Some Closing Thoughts

We all learn quickly that in order to accomplish anything with young people in a group setting, a certain amount of order must be created. The group must understand who is in charge and what kinds of behaviors are not acceptable.

The public ministry of Jesus shows us a better way. If you want to successfully lead young Christian disciples, just teach as Jesus did!

Think About . . .

1. How would you liken your own teaching style to that of Jesus?
2. In one sentence, what would you say was the message you wanted to share at a previous session? How can you summarize the message for an upcoming lesson in a few brief sentences? What are some ways to connect that central message to the lives of the young people?
3. Recall the last compassionate word or action you directed toward a young person or young people. What was the reaction? Consider how teaching with compassion can be a successful tool for leading young people.

Guests Are the Best

What do you remember most about the last party you attended? the music? the decorations? the food? or was it the people? Often what really makes a party special are the guests. More than cake or balloons, guests can be counted on to add an air of excitement, keep things interesting, and just make you feel good about being there.

Guests can do the same things for faith-formation sessions. They can dramatically change the routine and chemistry of a group and quickly succeed in pumping partylike energy and enthusiasm into a session. In this enlivened atmosphere, guests can share new religious experiences and a fresh breath of spiritual life. When guests serve up their personal message of faith in their unique style, you and the young people in your group will feel enriched, affirmed, and glad to have made these new acquaintances.

Choosing a Guest

Deciding to invite a guest and finding that guest are two very different things. To help narrow the search for potential visitors, consider the following four guidelines.

Choose a Guest Whose Message Enhances Your Own Teaching

Remember, you're not looking for someone to just provide entertainment or give you a break. What you really want is a guest who can bring a fresh point of view or has something substantial to add to the material you're covering. The guest's task is to use his or her education, training, and life experiences to provide the group with an expanded vision, a richer appreciation, or a deeper comprehension of the subject matter. So don't invite a guest just to invite a guest.

Choose a Guest Who Has Solid Communication Skills

Even the best message will be lost if the messenger struggles to share it. The need for clear communication, however, does not necessarily mean that a guest has to be a gifted public speaker. In fact, a guest may be someone who abandons formal speaking almost entirely and chooses to convey a message through music, drama, puppetry, art, a craft, poetry, or a story. In choosing a guest, you need to be convinced only that she or he can effectively translate a message through a medium the young people will understand. The best way to determine whether a potential guest will be able to do this is to see her or him in action or get input from others who have.

Choose a Guest Who Conveys His or Her Message with Conviction

Whatever the topic, whatever the means of communication, a guest must have energy and enthusiasm for his or her message or it will be ineffective. He or she may impart a story crisply and the young people may understand it completely, but if the guest doesn't share his or her message with passion, it will miss the mark. The more involved in and excited about the message a guest is, the more engaged the young people are likely to become.

Choose a Guest Who Enjoys Being with Young People

Look for someone who relates easily with young people without compromising discipline or respect. An ideal guest possesses a combination of sensitivity, generosity, and patience and attempts to gently include the inattentive and rein in the potentially disruptive. Most of all, an effective guest honestly and openly enjoys every moment of this shared experience.

Whom to Invite?

Of course, the perfect guest is far easier to imagine than to actually find. Where do you look to find that unique person who is willing and able to share a meaningful spiritual message in a youth-friendly manner? Everywhere. But start with the parish DRE, the CYM, and other parish staff members. These people can walk you through diocesan and regional resources or direct you to pastoral ministry centers at nearby Catholic colleges or high schools. Under their guidance, you may even want to check out speakers offered by secular nonprofit organizations, such as the Boys and Girls Clubs of America, the Red Cross, or Oxfam America.

Drawing from outside sources can be exciting, but you are just as likely to discover that the person you are looking for is right there in your own parish. Consider pastoral associates, others who serve in lay ministry positions, and interested parishioners. And don't overlook the talented pool of adults who are parents of the young people in parish programs. At your fingertips are highly visible people of faith with something valuable to share about prayer, the sacraments, vocations, service, and almost any aspect of faith.

Before you contact a potential guest, make certain you are prepared to discuss in clear, simple terms exactly what you are asking him or her to do. The guest will need to know such basics as the topic you want him or her to cover, how long you expected him or her to present, and the ages of the young people in the group. It is helpful to offer information about the setting, the availability of equipment, and additional specifics about your particular group.

The better you frame a guest's participation, the more effectively she or he will perform. Map out clearly how the guest's presentation fits into the overall teaching plan. Do you want your guest to introduce a new topic or enrich one that you've already covered? What were you discussing in previous sessions? What will you move on to in future sessions? Consider how the guest can contribute to this flow of information.

In fairness, and for best results, it is equally important that you give the young people adequate advanced notice of the upcoming visit. Also discuss with the group appropriate behavior and respectful appreciation for the efforts of any guest.

Getting ready may also mean helping the group learn a little bit about their guest by sharing relevant biographical information, either verbally or in written form. Give the young people a chance to express their own expectations about the upcoming visit. Why do they think you have invited this person to their meeting? What special abilities or gifts do they think this guest might possess? What questions would they like to ask this person? This kind of pre-visit sharing can help the young people look forward to meeting the guest not as an unexpected intruder but as someone who has come with an important message just for them.

It's in the Details

As the group leader, you are likely to have a few details to attend to yourself. You'll want to be sure the meeting space is appropriately prepared and that you are ready to offer a welcoming introduction that can quickly connect the guest to the group. You may want to give some forethought to how you can assist the guest in maintaining discipline during the presentation if need be. And don't ignore the possibility that, despite your excellent preparation, everything might not go according to plan. It never hurts to have some backup material in case a guest comes late, finishes early, or doesn't show up at all.

The more you prepare, the easier it will be for you to relax and enjoy the guest you have invited.

Some Closing Thoughts

Picture the expressions on the young people's faces when a guest sings an outrageous song or tells a remarkable, but true, story. Imagine your own amazement when the most reluctant student asks an unbelievably insightful question. What's moving a few chairs and making a few phone calls compared to the joy of seeing the young people put their best selves forward, or watching the spirit-driven interaction of a special adult with equally special young people? When it comes to enlivening and enriching a religious education or faith-sharing session, guests are the best.

Think About . . .

1. Think about the last party or get-together you attended. Of the guests present, who stands out the most in your memory of that event? Why?
2. Think of the best guest presenters you have witnessed. What made them so effective? What special techniques or teaching devices did they use?
3. Consider the theme of the last lesson you led. How might a guest have enriched that session?
4. With the DRE, the CYM, other volunteers, or by yourself, consider remaining lesson themes for this year. Then discuss or think about where and when you might incorporate a guest most effectively.

Teach Me a Story

Everyone loves a good story, but stories can be more than simple crowd-pleasers. Catechist and ministry volunteers can use stories as subtle aids to add variety and enduring meaning to any faith-sharing session.

Like the unexpected arrival of an old friend, a well-chosen story can bring welcomed variety to a session and elevate everyone's interest and enthusiasm. When you tell a story, you automatically change your sharing landscape by introducing new characters for the group to meet and get to know—characters that go places, do things, and are seldom dull. Long, short, funny, sad, frightening, or mysterious, stories are never the same. This unpredictability is what excites the young people's curiosity, draws them in, and holds their attention until the end.

At faith-sharing sessions, stories can also serve as vehicles of enduring meaning. Young people consistently remember the things that touch their imagination, connect with their interests, or stir their emotions. If asked, the young people will read pages 15–20 and answer questions 6–10. But in the end, it is the story you share that they will hold on to, squirrel away, and then tell anew to friends and family. It's the story that lasts.

You can begin to use this many-faceted tool at your very next session. No matter what the topic, the lesson will undoubtedly have three easily identifiable parts—a beginning, a middle, and an end. Stories can help you teach more effectively at each juncture.

Stories at the Beginning

For the young people, the hours that directly precede a faith-sharing session can be filled with complicated collections of people, experiences, and emotions. When a session begins, it can take you lots of valuable time and energy just to get everyone settled and on task. Surprisingly enough, stories can help *you* transition too. Telling a story at the outset of a session can help you refuel after your own trying or tiring day. Telling a story can help you energize yourself for the remainder of the session.

As an introductory tool, stories not only mesmerize the young people and energize a leader but also effectively draw everyone together and point to what lies ahead. An opening story about a lost dog can lead to a message about the joy of reconciliation; a tale of gold and treasure to a discussion of Christian values; or an epic of courage and adventure to a lesson about the first Christians. Getting a story out early provides you and the group with a shared point of understanding that can serve as a reference point throughout a session.

Stories in the Middle

As a session progresses, you and the young people can find yourselves moving in opposite directions. The young people may want to turn away from the monotony of reading, writing, and discussing even though you're bravely trying to move ahead and stay on message. Stories can help resolve this sometimes predictable impasse. When the young people hear the opening lines of a story, they automatically relax. Used in the middle of a lesson, a story can be the hinge, the glue, or even the centerpiece of an entire lesson.

Stories at the End

You may choose to save a story until the closing minutes of a session, when it can serve multiple purposes. If you need to put the brakes on sliding attention and behavior as a lesson winds down, tell a story. If you want to summarize the lesson in a subtle way that doesn't involve review questions or vocabulary words, tell a story. If you want the young people to leave the session with a smile and something special to share at home, tell a story.

Finding a Good Story

Of course, no matter where it is set, the real success of a story depends on how good it is and how well you present it. Fortunately, good stories abound in the Scriptures, in movies, on television shows, in resource books, and in daily life experiences. But not every good story is the right story for your group or your faith-sharing session.

Narrowing down the options means first selecting a story that is age-appropriate. Consider these kinds of questions:

- Does the story use words that are within the comprehension of the young people, or is the vocabulary too advanced or stilted?
- Does the story center on concepts or themes that are familiar to the young people, or are the ideas obviously geared for another age level?

- Is this story one the young people could easily put into their own words and share with someone else?

The stories you want to choose are those that help bring the meaning of the day's lesson into the lives of the young people or that allow you to illustrate or explore the lesson more fully. If a story doesn't relate easily to the lesson, you need to find a different story. Complete your selection process by searching for stories that are age-appropriate, relevant, and enjoyable.

Once you have chosen a story, you might think your job is done. But even the best story is only as good as how it is presented. The good news is that you don't have to be a professional storyteller to use stories effectively with young people.

If you are comfortable reading or telling a story, that's fine. But don't overlook all the other possibilities. You can share a story through a movie or an audiotape. Why not try using a script that will encourage the group to dramatize the tale? Familiar stories might be retold with each person adding to the story around a circle. You can share wonderful stories through song, rap, rhyme, or mime. The possibilities are endless.

Some Closing Thoughts

There's no question that using stories as a faith-sharing device is likely to involve some planning. It takes time to find a story that advances your message and connects with the group, and even more time to decide how to place and present the story effectively in a lesson. But you may be more willing to make that extra effort when you read this little story:

> Once there was a carpenter's son who told a wonderful story to his friends. They were so moved and improved by the story that they told it to their

> friends and family. Their friends and family were so moved and improved that they rephrased it a bit and retold it to their friends and so on and so on.

Motivated yet?

Think About . . .

1. Reflect on memorable stories you heard from teachers, family members, or friends. Why are these stories memorable to you?
2. How in touch are you with your own collection of faith stories? Recall or discuss with others one or more stories from your own spiritual journey that might enrich lessons about prayer, faith, liturgy, service, or the sacraments.
3. When was the last time you started or ended a session with a story? How successful was the story as a teaching tool? What changes in the story selection, placement, or delivery might have made it more effective?

8 And Now Let Us Pray

The Lord's Prayer is a spiritual treasure. It is the prayer that Jesus taught the Apostles and the prayer that sustained early Christian communities. It is a prayer that has weathered Church division and a prayer that continues to connect Christians around the world today.

Whether or not young people are aware of its considerable history, most know the Lord's Prayer. In fact, many young people approach the prayer with a certain sense of ownership, because they have prayed it at home, at Mass, and at faith-sharing sessions for as long as they can remember.

It is precisely because young people are so comfortable and at ease with the Lord's Prayer that catechist and ministry volunteers can use it as a unique teaching tool. By providing prayer experiences that place the familiar words of the Lord's Prayer into a variety of prayer formats, you can gently open the door for the young people in your group to confidently explore and experience new ways to pray.

Tweaking the Traditional Prayer Mode

At faith-sharing sessions, a common format for praying the Lord's Prayer is to simply recite it as a group. Before a session starts, or at its closing, the young people stand, sit, or kneel and join in praying the memorized words aloud together.

Minor changes in that basic prayer format can substantially alter the experience for the young people. For example, you might assign yourself or a group member to pray the words of the Lord's Prayer aloud while the rest of the group shares the words silently in their hearts. Freed from the action of speaking the prayer, the young people can receive the words of the prayer as listeners and experience it anew through the prism of another's vocal expression.

You might prefer to divide the vocalization of the prayer among the young people by asking each person to pray one phrase of the prayer as the recitation moves around the table or room. The first young person says "Our Father who art in heaven," the second follows with "hallowed be thy name," and so on until the end of the prayer. The added touch of dimming the lights in the room and then passing a lighted candle from speaker to speaker during the prayer can help slow the pace of the prayer and allow the young people to focus attention on each individual phrase. This simple rotation of participants encourages the young people to both concentrate on the phrases they speak and absorb the meaning of the rest of the prayer slowly, phrase by phrase.

A third minor tweaking of the traditional praying of the Lord's Prayer requires sufficient space to divide and relocate the group around the meeting space in pairs. Instruct the pairs to pray the Lord's Prayer on their own cue, together, in hushed voices. It is unlikely that many of the young people have prayed in this exact configuration or in tandem like this before. Praying the Lord's Prayer in this way makes the words seem less institutional and more personal, and it gives the young people a unique experience of belonging to an intimate community of prayer.

Silent Prayer

The young people live in a world where the volume is continually being pumped up. They may actually be relieved to hear you announce:

† Today we will close our lesson by praying the Lord's Prayer silently. Please close your eyes, take a deep breath, and as you exhale, try to let go of whatever has troubled you today. Replace those concerns with thoughts of God. Now, at your own pace, pray the words of the Lord's Prayer silently in your mind and heart.

When you feel enough time has elapsed, ask the young people to open their eyes. Then conclude the session.

A second silent alternative allows the young people to experience a mantra, or centering approach. Prior to a session, divide the Lord's Prayer into phrases suitable for reflection such as "lead us not into temptation," "forgive us our trespasses," or "give us this day our daily bread," and print these phrases on a chalkboard, whiteboard, or sheet of newsprint. Share the following instructions with the group:

† Today, instead of praying the entire Lord's Prayer, you will have the chance to reflect on one small part of it. Please choose one of the phrases on the board. Close your eyes and now silently and slowly repeat the phrase you selected over and over again in your mind and heart as your own personal prayer.

Allow time appropriate to the group.

Not all silent prayer needs to be meditative or performed with eyes closed. To try a different style of silent prayer, distribute a pencil and sheet of paper to each young person. Then ask the group to write, without regard to perfect spelling or punctuation, the words of the Lord's Prayer, praying the words silently as they write them. When they have finished writing the entire prayer, they should return to the beginning and silently pray through the prayer one more time.

Praying in Another Language

Thanks to television specials and minicourses at school, today many young people are well acquainted with, and often genuinely fascinated by, the special language of the hearing impaired. For young people with unimpaired hearing, learning to express the words of the Lord's Prayer through the unique medium of finger spelling or American Sign Language can place a fresh filter on the words of the prayer and add new dimensions to their prayer life. You may not be equipped to provide this experience yourself, but you can check with the DRE or CYM to find out if there are young people or adults in your parish program who are willing and able to facilitate this prayer opportunity. You might also consider doing some Internet research to find the necessary instructions for praying the Lord's Prayer in American Sign Language.

Music may not be recognized as a language in its own right, but setting the words of the Lord's Prayer to music definitely alters the way listeners experience the prayer. For example, listening to a group of people sing the Lord's Prayer slowly with heavy melody lines might lead some of the young people to greater reflection on the words of the prayer, while hearing the same words sung against an upbeat tempo may simply inspire others to prayerfully rejoice in their faith.

The young people may not initially want to sing the Lord's Prayer themselves, but they may welcome the chance to hear recordings of various sung versions and pray along. With some direction, they might even select a group favorite and eventually surprise you by joining in. Your DRE or CYM can help you find appropriate materials and equipment.

Finally, you might want to include in prayer experiences praying the Lord's Prayer in the language the young people like best—their own. This prayer activity may require some investment of time initially, but once you complete that initial preparation, the activity will be easy to conduct in the future. Your direction might sound like this:

† When Jesus taught the Apostles the Lord's Prayer, he used words that were in common usage at the time. Today we are going to try to translate the Lord's Prayer into the language we use and perhaps understand more clearly today. Work in pairs or groups of three to update a few phrases of the prayer. [Divide the phrases of the prayer among the groups.] The goal is to change the words of the original prayer to make them sound more like the language we use today, without losing the real meaning of the original prayer.

When the groups are finished, put the newly written phrases together to form a complete prayer that the group can then say together. By saving and reproducing this translation of the Lord's Prayer, you have a "homemade" prayer option to be used whenever you wish.

Some Closing Thoughts

As catechist and ministry volunteers, we pray with young people all the time. We want them to feel comfortable and to grow spiritually from the prayer experiences we share. The Lord's Prayer provides us with an exceptional teaching tool to help achieve both of these goals.

Think About . . .

1. How do you ordinarily pray with the young people at faith-sharing sessions? How frequently do you say the Lord's Prayer?
2. Have you previously tried silent prayer methods in faith-sharing sessions? How did the young people react? Of the silent prayer samples presented in this chapter, which would you be most likely to try?
3. Plan at least one alternative prayer experience that makes creative use of the Lord's Prayer.

Session Savers

For nearly an hour, the young people have been reading and discussing, listening and responding. As the leader, you have been swept along by the joy of a lesson gone right. Then with about ten minutes remaining in the session, as if on cue, some of the young people begin to spontaneously disengage. Fingers start tapping, feet make restless sliding noises on the floor, eyes dart anxiously from clock to door. The euphoria of the first 50 minutes is about to dissolve into the disorder of the last 10.

Sound familiar? It's happened to all of us. But before it happens to you again, consider the three session-saving alternatives that follow. Each option is easy to plan and simple to share. Each enables you to recapture the attention and enthusiasm of the group and bring the lesson to a productive close.

Have I Got Something for You!

You may correctly recognize this closing activity as a handy review tool, but the young people are more likely to view it as a welcomed change of pace accented by an element of surprise.

You will want to prepare for this exercise by creating a grab bag filled with words or objects that are clearly related to the lesson for the day. On small slips of paper, write the words you select and then fold the slips in half. If you decide to use objects, they should be small, lightweight household items. The bag should be large enough to accommodate the contents and for the group to easily see. Colorful shopping bags or party bags work well.

When the time is right, introduce this closing exercise by saying something like, "We are going to complete the session with an activity called 'Have I Got Something for You!'" Simultaneously reveal the grab bag so the young people believe you really *do* have something for them. Then explain that in turn, each young person will be invited to take an object or word from the bag. He or she will then have 30 seconds to explain how the word or object is related to the lesson. If necessary, the young person can request the help of one other group member.

Ask for a volunteer to go first and then explain how the rest of the young people will know when it is their turn (the next person around the circle, chosen by the person who had the last turn, chosen randomly by you, and so on). Now you are ready to start.

As the activity proceeds, you can facilitate by reinforcing suitable responses, rephrasing those that miss the mark, and keeping the activity moving and on track until the end of the session.

This activity can be dressed up and varied according to the tastes of the young people in the group. You can alter its dynamic by choosing teams and making it competitive. You might award small prizes or treats for appropriate responses. Another way to vary the activity is to ask the participants to either illustrate or act out the word or object for the group to guess.

Get the Picture

Come armed with markers, drawing paper, and a little imagination to deliver this hands-on session closer. With about 10 minutes remaining in the session, distribute one marker and one sheet of paper to each young person. Ask them to close their eyes while you offer these instructions:

- † Try to picture in your mind the things we talked about in today's lesson. [If necessary, give a few suggestions.] In a moment, I will ask you to open your eyes and remain silent. When you do, use your marker to draw and title a picture that illustrates any part of today's lesson. Don't worry about the quality of your artwork. Stick figures are acceptable. Do not sign your name. Without any conversation, open your eyes and begin.

When time has expired, collect the artwork and share as time allows. You might also use the artwork at the beginning of the next session to help connect the lessons if they are sequential.

As an alternative, you might refine your request by asking for sketches of more specific parts of a lesson. Or, if time allows, briefly describe major themes of the next lesson and ask for accompanying illustrations. Allowing the young people to express themselves in this artistic and relaxing way not only saves the session but is likely to provide you with creative focus and review materials for the future.

What Difference Does It Make?

If the young people are ready for a real challenge, you may want to polish off some lessons with this interactive exercise. Begin by offering the following introduction:

† During the session time today, we could have been at home watching television, talking on the phone, surfing the Internet, or even taking a nap. But instead we spent most of this hour talking and thinking about the Beatitudes [substitute the theme for the lesson]. Now let's see if our time was well spent.

Direct the young people to work in small groups and then share an instruction like this:

† Take a few minutes to determine both *if* and *how* learning about the Beatitudes today can make a difference in the way you will live your life tomorrow and in the future. We will share the results of your small group discussion in a few minutes.

Share the responses as time permits.

A standard variation of this activity is to ask the young people to consider who, besides themselves, might benefit from this lesson. Another variation is to ask the young people to work in pairs or small groups to determine what part of this lesson might be helpful to a friend, their parents, people in positions of authority, or people who are in trouble.

Turning over the last 10 minutes of a session to this type of discussion can release energy and direct conversation into productive channels by encouraging the young people to place the day's message into the context of daily living.

Some Closing Thoughts

As with any faith-sharing tool, session savers are meant to be used sparingly and in rotation. When you do reach for that special closing activity, you'll want to select one that significantly contrasts with the kind of participation the group has been experiencing for most of the lesson. For example, the drawing required by "Get the Picture" is likely to be a welcome change after a session filled with discussion, but it could fall flat if you tried to work it in at the end of a major craft or art project. Group work required by "What Difference Does It Make?" could be the perfect antidote for the tedium of lots of individual reading and writing, but it won't accomplish anything if you use it after another similar small-group activity.

Fortunately, not every lesson requires saving. In fact, with creative preparation and careful time management, you can expect most lessons to flow smoothly and fit neatly into the allotted time. But for those occasions during every year when, for whatever reason, youthful attention wanes, enthusiasm dwindles, and the final ten minutes of a gathering seem ready to stretch on forever, don't panic and don't stress out—just reach for a session saver.

Think About . . .

1. When was the last time you were in need of a session saver? How did the young people indicate they were beginning to disconnect with the lesson? What did you do?
2. Which sample activity would you be most comfortable using? Which do you think is most appealing to young people?
3. Look ahead to a future lesson. What words or household objects would you put in the grab bag if you wanted to try "Have I Got Something for You!"?

Leading by Following

Is your enthusiasm for the faith sometimes overcome by anxiety about your ability to share it? Do you suddenly wish you had taken more faith development or leadership training classes? Do you question your supply of patience, flexibility, or humor? Are you concerned about teaching without the gift of a commanding voice, a no-nonsense manner, or well-honed organization skills? Relax. You can effectively use the God-given talents you do possess and lead with confidence if, first, you can agree to be a follower.

Follow the Leader

Most parishes place their faith-sharing programs under the supervision of a professionally trained DRE or CYM. He or she is responsible for maintaining the continuity, integrity, strength, and effectiveness of the complete parish program to and with young people. The DRE or CYM routinely reviews, selects, and organizes texts, resources, and activities appropriate for each learning level. His or her job, at least in part, is to make sure your faith-sharing assignment is manageable.

But the best plans and intentions of parish leaders succeed only if you commit yourself to following them. Your responsibility, then, is not to rewrite or reassemble the program, but rather to do your very best to present material in the order and with the emphasis suggested. Disregarding experienced leadership can effectively disconnect you and the young people from the support, authenticity, and cohesion that come from being part of an organized, professionally prepared program.

Of course, it is not unusual for catechist and ministry volunteers to be tempted to depart from a prepared lesson plan. It is sometimes easy to convince yourself that another topic might be more important, more fun, or more in tune with what the young people want to hear. Off-topic faith sharing may initially seem liberating for both you and the young people, but freelancing your way through a faith-sharing session is like walking a tightrope without a net. It won't take long for you to feel tense, off balance, and ready for a fall.

On the other hand, sticking to the plan allows both you and the group you are guiding to feel a sense of order and accomplishment as you complete each lesson. The more familiar you become with working from a plan, the more relaxed and comfortable you will be sharing the faith with the young people.

Before each session, read through the session plan and try to picture the process happening with the group. You may need to make some adjustments based on your knowledge of the young people and the actual physical setting. Some activities will require preparation. This could range from copying a list onto a sheet of newsprint to creating game pieces or finding photographs. Allowing yourself adequate preparation time is essential. All sessions typically include brief periods where you share Church teachings. Spend time putting these presentations together so they are clear and hold the attention of the young people. And remember, where it is helpful and appropriate, share parts of your own story with the young people.

As you move through lessons from week to week, you will build confidence for yourself and understanding for the young people because you will be using professionally prepared and sequenced materials that allow the young people to learn in ways that are appropriate for their age and development level. Following the direction of the DRE or CYM will allow you to be an effective leader yourself.

Follow Your Gifts

As much as a DRE or CYM might encourage you to follow "the plan," you are not meant to simply perform as a robot. There is room and reason in every faith-sharing program for catechist and ministry volunteers to share the faith creatively. While adhering to the lesson plans, you can effectively lead faith-sharing sessions in a unique way by following the call of your own skills, talents, and personality traits. For instance, do you have a kid-tested sense of humor? Do you enjoy telling stories? Do you have a flare for photography, an interest in drama, or an unusual music collection? What part of *you* can you bring to faith sharing? The fact that you can draw or sing or dance gives you the opportunity not to abandon the message but to find your own individual point of connection with the young people as you attempt to share that message.

By following the call of your own special gifts, you can bring a lesson to life. A lesson about Baptism takes on freshness and vitality when it is accompanied by family photos of the Baptism of your son or daughter. The meaning of Christian service can be fleshed out by a story you tell about your own teen experiences at a homeless shelter or senior center. The feeling of forgiveness that comes through the sacrament of Penance and Reconciliation may be transmitted on a whole different level by a suitable CD from your personal collection.

It will take only a few such attempts for you to prove to yourself that following your gifts can provide you with a new and unique dimension to your leadership style, one that can personalize and double the impact of any lesson you set out to teach.

Follow the Young People

At every age, young people provide countless clues about who they are and how they learn. Patiently listening for and then following those hints can help you lead faith-sharing sessions that are relevant and memorable for you and the group.

With resources provided by your DRE or CYM, you can learn about the distinctive characteristics of the age-group with which you are working. Forewarned is definitely forearmed. You will begin to correctly interpret some of their actions as par for the course. Instead of consistently faulting yourself, you will find it possible to occasionally shrug your shoulders, smile, and move on.

This kind of general knowledge provides great assistance, but you should also get to know the young people as individuals. Begin to discover who they are and what is happening in their lives by tuning in to their culture—books, movies, music—and by listening carefully to their questions, responses, and conversations before, during, and after the sessions. Give importance to their thoughts, ideas, and concerns by incorporating them into your lessons as examples or starting points for discussion.

In this way, a lesson about Jesus and the Apostles might begin with a short discussion about the strengths and weaknesses of the young people's own groups of friends. The unlimited love and forgiveness of God the Father may compute better for young minds if you compare it to the love and forgiveness of familiar father figures they know from television shows or movies. You can effectively introduce an understanding of faith commitment by comparing it to the young people's commitment to sports, music, or drama.

Follow Christ

To a large degree, the level of respectful attention you can command and the overall success you can expect in leading faith discussions will depend on how believable you are. You create that credibility not only by the truth of what you teach but also by the integrity with which you teach it.

Young people are very perceptive students of human behavior and are incredibly adept at spotting those who aren't at least *trying* to practice what they preach. They are suspicious of English teachers who consistently make errors in grammar or music teachers who can't keep the beat.

The young people you work with will be watching you as well, and in their own way, they will be gauging the sincerity of your faith. It will not be enough for you to talk to them about how to be loving, caring, and forgiving if they do not see you attempting to be those things as well. They will not expect you to be a saint, but they will accept leadership best from you if you appear to be working hard to follow the Lord Jesus.

Some Closing Thoughts

Following the plans laid out for you by your DRE or CYM can keep you on task. Responding to the call of your own gifts and abilities can enrich your presentation. Allowing the subtle suggestions of the young people to flavor your approach will help you to be relevant. But in the end, to effectively lead faith sharing-sessions with the young people, you must give them visible proof of your daily attempt to follow Christ and to become the message you teach.

Think About . . .

1. What special skills, talents, and personality traits would your spouse or best friend say you have? How might you use those skills, talents, or traits in a faith-sharing setting?
2. What do you think are three outstanding characteristics of the age-group with which you work? How can those traits bring positive effects as well as challenges into a faith-sharing situation?
3. How might the young people react to your faith-sharing sessions after seeing you with your family at Mass? hearing you gossip about other parents? watching you quietly help a young person who is struggling with a problem?